ALL CHORDS
in ALL POSITIONS
FOR GUITAR

by Muriel Anderson

See page 79 for MOVEABLE CHORD GUIDE.

ISBN 978-0-7935-6259-6

HAL•LEONARD®
CORPORATION
7777 W. BLUEMOUND RD. P.O. BOX 13819 MILWAUKEE, WI 53213

Visit Hal Leonard on the internet at http://www.halleonard.com

ALL CHORDS
IN ALL POSITIONS
FOR GUITAR

INTRODUCTION

This book presents a different way of learning chords. By defining and constructing them in all areas of the fingerboard, you will understand the system behind chord construction as well as discover different ways of making each chord. You are encouraged to play with the examples given and explore other possibilities on your own.

Once you have completed the diagrams, they can be used for reference as you need them. All possible inversions of each type of chord are contained in the diagrams, provided the guitar is in standard tuning (E-A-D-G-B-E; low to high).

Fingerings
In this book, any way the left hand can finger the chords is acceptable. In fact, practice making the chords several different ways to find the most practical way to move from one chord to the next in a song.

You may consult the glossary in the back of the book for definitions of terms used in chord construction.

Once you have constructed the chord forms in "C" position as given in the following pages, you can use the moveable chord guide to find all other chords. All shape relationships remain the same for all keys.

There are blank chord diagrams in the back of this book to use as you like.

All Chords In All Positions is designed as a workbook—a vehicle to find chords on the guitar and experiment with them on your own. So, take out your pencils...

Let's start with a regular C chord. As you look at the notes that you are playing, notice that they are all Cs, Es, and Gs:

You can also think of these as the 1st, 3rd, and 5th notes of the C major scale:

Look at a G major chord. All the notes are Gs, Bs, Ds, or 1, 3, and 5 of the G major scale:

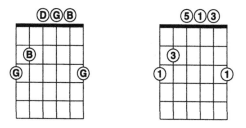

Play other major chords you know. You will find that the notes are all firsts, thirds, and fifths of that major scale.

So... It would stand to reason that if you circled all the 1s, 3s, and 5s in the C major scale, you would get every possible way to make a C major chord—by definition! Let's try it

* (Note: Don't confuse the scale degree numbers with fingering numbers. Remember: any chord in this book may be played with any possible left hand fingering.)

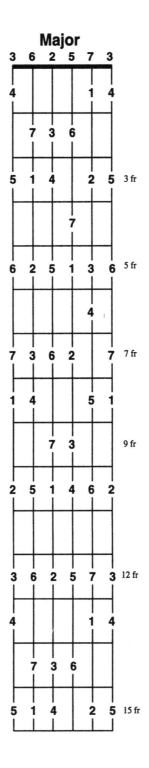

(Written: C, C Major, C Maj)

Directions:

Here are the notes of the C major scale. The **major chord** is made up of 1, 3, and 5 of the major scale. Any number of 1s, 3s, or 5s, in any octave may be used. Circle all scale degrees 1, 3, and 5. The result is a single large chord diagram containing all the possible ways to play a C Major chord.

Experiment to see how many different ways you can make the C major chord. Be sure the chord has at least one of each of the scale degrees 1, 3, and 5. Some combinations of notes (shapes or inversions) are easier to make than others.

Connect the circles with lines, like constellations, to make the shapes easier to visualize. You can use different colors to indicate different positions or different scale degrees.

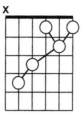

Notice that this big chord diagram contains the shape of every major chord you've ever made (provided the guitar is in standard tuning).

Memory Aid:
The major scale as we know it, evolved from combining two identical four note scales, called *tetrachords*. The term "tetrachord" means "four strings" as some of the earliest stringed instruments were four-string lyres (as the angels play on Christmas cards...). The intervals between the notes in each of these particular tetrachords are: whole step, whole step, half step. Combining two of these tetrachords with a whole step between yields the major scale. Think of two angels getting together for a jam session:

MAJOR SCALE CONSTRUCTION – Exercise

Start on any note. Go up the fingerboard using the major scale formula of whole steps and half steps. The result will be the major scale based upon that first note. Wherever the notes fall using this formula determines what sharps or flats occur in the given key. The scale will have one of each letter name from A to G (although some may be sharped or flatted). The C major scale (using this formula starting on a C note) has no sharps or flats. (See *A Look at Scale Construction,* page 58.)

Okay, let's try the same thing with the G major scale!

Major Chord: 1, 3, 5

G Major

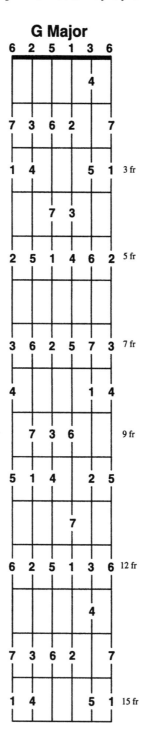

Directions:

Circle all scale degrees 1, 3, and 5 in the G major scale. The result is a single large chord diagram containing all the possible ways to play a G major chord.

Notice that the shapes of the chords are the same as the big C major chord diagram, but starting on a different fret.

In essence, this demonstrates how the moveable chord guide works.

Because the distances between the notes are the same for major scales, you really only need one diagram to find all the major chords in all positions (see *Moving Chords and Scale Construction* on pages 57-58).

Devil's advocate: "So you're telling me that I didn't need to do this G major scale diagram at all?"

Exactly. You can start anywhere on any major scale diagram and imagine that the guitar neck begins there. The same sequence of shapes will follow. For example, to make the G major scale from the C major scale diagram, cover up the first five frets of the diagram, and presto!—there's the G major scale. Whichever note that scale degree "1" falls on is the name of your new scale. Any chord built upon that scale follows the same patterns. The *Moveable Chord Guide* on p. 79 makes it easier to visualize. (See index: *Moving the entire diagram* on p. 56. There are many ways to use this information)

As a reference, the scale degree numbers of the C major scale are indicated on all the fingerboard charts on the following pages. The numbers above the diagrams are the scale degree numbers of the open strings. Think of the open strings as fret number zero.

All chords for each diagram may be found by using the *Moveable Chord Guide* on page 79.

Memory Aid: Chord Shapes
If you are familiar with first position chords, you will recognize—as you move up the neck—chord shapes which resemble C-A-G-E-D. Above the twelfth fret the shapes repeat themselves. All major chords follow the same shape relationship. A good way to remember the shapes as you move up the neck is that they spell the word "CAGED." As you start at the twelfth fret and move down to the first fret you can see all major shapes in order: C-D-E-F-G-A-B-C. (The chord shapes overlap). Memorize the order in which these shapes progress up and down the fingerboard. (You don't need to play all of the notes in each shape. For example, on the G-shape, you may choose to play just the top four strings.)

Chord Forms
(C-A-G-E-D)

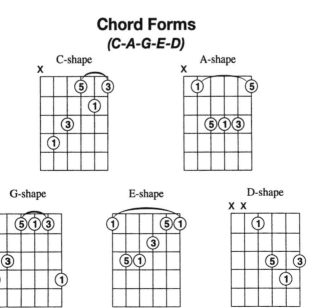

Minor Chord: 1, ♭3, 5

Minor

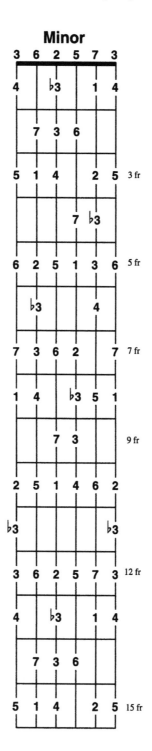

[Written: Cm, Cmin, C-, or c (lower case letter)]

Directions:
Circle all scale degrees 1, ♭3, and 5 (♭3 is located on the fret between 2 and 3). This will give you all possible C minor chords.

You can think of the complete *minor chord diagram* as the *major chord diagram*, with all the "3s" moved back one fret.

Example:
E major changes to E minor:

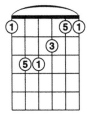

Root in the 6th string ("E-shape"):

Major   minor

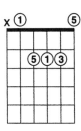

A major changes to A minor:

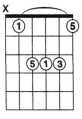

Root in the 5th string ("A-shape"):

Memory Aid:
You can remember where 3 is in any chord shape by thinking about which note moves back one fret when changing from major to minor.

Moving Chord Shapes:
Use the Em chord shape to find any minor chord, simply by moving the chord shape up or down the fingerboard. Again, the "1" on the 6th string determines the letter name of the chord.

Moving the Entire Diagram to Find All Minor Chord Shapes:
You can use the diagram on the left to find all the minor chords. If you move the entire diagram up one fret you will have all the C♯ minor chords. If you move the diagram down one fret you will have all the B minor chords. The pattern is the same for all minor chords, provided that "1" falls on the name of the chord.

For more information on minor chords, see *Another Way to Look at the Minor Chord Diagram* on page 62.

Dominant Seventh Chord: 1, 3, 5, ♭7

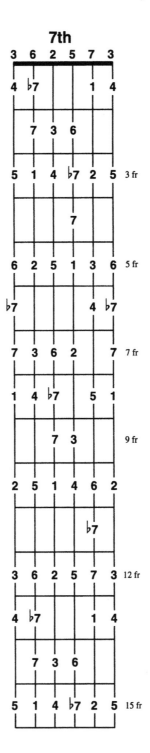

(Written: C7)

Directions:
Circle 1, 3, 5, and ♭7 (the space between 6 and 7). This gives you all possible C dominant seventh chords.

The term "dominant" means the chord built upon the fifth note of the scale (see *harmonized scale,* page 65). The dominant seventh chord contains a dissonance (from the 3 to the ♭7) which wants to resolve inward (a half step each). This is why the dominant seventh chord tends to resolve to the chord a perfect fifth lower (G7 goes to C, C7 goes to F, etc.). This principle is so integral to all of western music that we often omit the term "dominant" and simply call this type of chord "seventh."

It is particularly helpful to connect the circles with lines, like constellations, because it is impossible to play all the available notes in a given postion. It is necessary to make some choices: find the root, 1 (in the bass), at least one 3, one 5, and one ♭7. You may use 3, 5, or ♭7 in the bass to form an inversion.

Option: 5 may be left out. 1 identifies the name of the chord, 3 identifies the chord as a type of major chord (instead of ♭3, which would be minor), ♭7 identifies the chord as a dominant seventh, but 5 is not as crucial to identify the chord, so it may be left out.

You can think of the seventh chord as a major chord with one of the 1s moved back two frets.

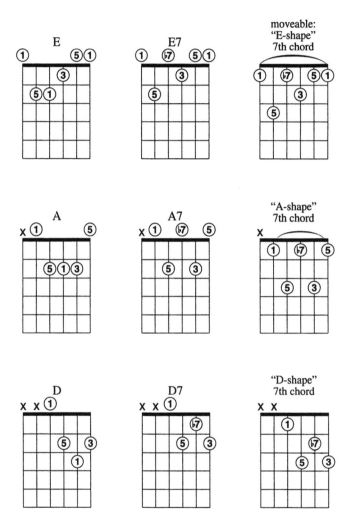

As mentioned earlier, the seventh chord wants to resolve to a chord a fifth lower. If you organize chords in fifths, you can create an infinite series of seventh chords that each resolve to the next chord. Turn to the circle of fifths on page 59 and move counter-clockwise around the circle, making each letter name a seventh chord (B7→E7→A7→D7→G7→ C7→F7→B♭7→E♭7→A♭7→D♭7→G♭7→B7...). You eventually go completely around the circle.

[Practice: See the *12-bar blues* on page 67.]

Major Seventh Chord: 1, 3, 5, 7

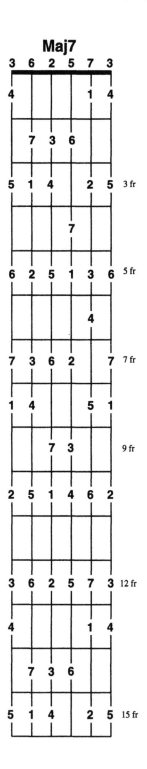

(Written: Cmaj7, CMa7, CM7, or C∆7)

Directions:

Circle 1, 3, 5, and 7. This gives you all possible C major seventh chords. For easy visualization, connect the circles to form "constellations;" chords containing the root 1 (in the bass), at least one 3, one 5, and one 7.

Options: 5 can be left out. You may use 3, 5, or 7 in the bass to make an inversion.

You can think of the major seventh chord as a seventh chord with the ♭7 moved up one fret, or as a major chord with one of the 1s moved back one fret:

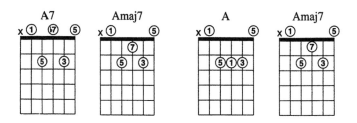

Major seventh and major ninth chords both make rich, jazzy substitutions for major chords.

Here are some common major seventh chords. Find them on the diagram that you have completed on the left.

(root on E string)
"E-shape" maj7

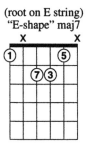

(root on A string)
"A-shape" maj7

(root on D string)
"D-shape" maj7

maj7

Minor Seventh Chord: 1, ♭3, 5, ♭7

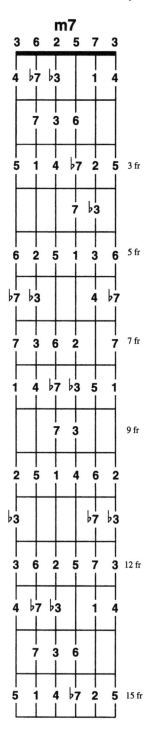

(Written: Cm7, Cmin7, or C-7)

Directions:

Circle 1, ♭3, 5, and ♭7. This gives you all possible minor seventh chords. Connect the circles to form "constellations" containing the root 1 (in the bass), at least one ♭3, one 5 and one ♭7.

Options: 5 may be left out. You may use ♭3, 5, or ♭7 in the bass to form inversions.

The minor seventh chord is a nice substitute for a regular minor. Practice making minor chords in several positions, then transfrom the chord into a minor seventh by adding the ♭7 (or moving one of the 1s back two frets).

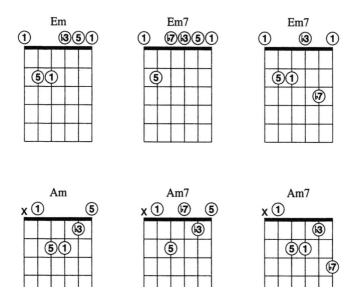

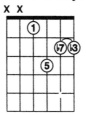

Find these minor seventh shapes on the diagram to the left:

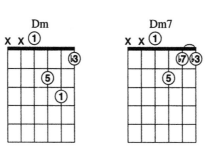

Minor Seventh Flat Five or Half-Diminished Seventh Chord:
1, ♭3, ♭5, ♭7

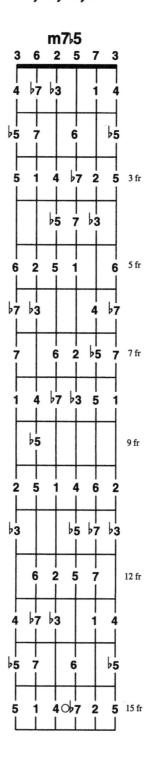

(Written: Cm7-5, Cm7♭5, C-7(♭5), or Cᵒ7)

Directions:

Circle 1, ♭3, ♭5, and ♭7. This gives you all possible C minor seventh flat five (or C half-diminished seventh) chords. Connect the circles to form "constellations" containing the root, 1 (in the bass), at least one ♭3, one ♭5, and one ♭7.

Options: ♭5 is often used in the bass. You may also use ♭3 or ♭7 in the bass to form other inversions.

Compare the shapes to the minor sixth chord (page 34).

Slash Chords

The letter following a slash mark is simply the bass note for the chord. For example, C7/G is the C7 chord with a G note in the bass. It may be played like this:

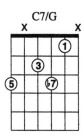

Here is a progression using minor seventh flat five chords as passing chords between seventh and minor seventh chords. Notice the seventh chords with the fifth of the chord in the bass (bass note indicated behind the slash).

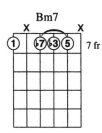

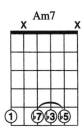

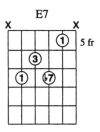

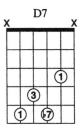

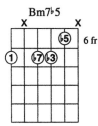

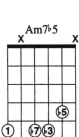

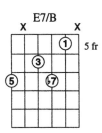

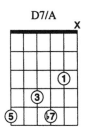

Seventh Flat Five Chord: 1, 3, ♭5, ♭7

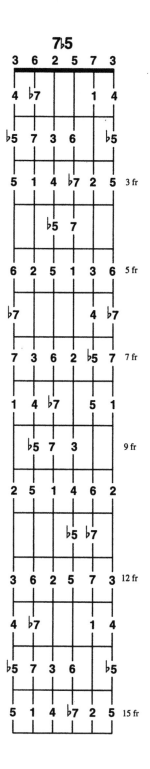

(Written: C7♭5, C7(♭5), or C7-5)

Directions:

Circle 1, 3, ♭5, and ♭7. This gives you all possible C seventh flat five chords. Connect the circles to form "constellations" containing the root, 1 (in the bass), at least one 3, one ♭5 and one ♭7. Options: ♭5 is often used in the bass. You may also use 3 or ♭7 in the bass to form other inversions.

You may notice that the shapes repeat themselves every six frets. This is because the interval relationship is somewhat symmetrical: the distance from scale degrees 1 to 3 is four frets, the same as ♭5 to ♭7. The distance from 3 to ♭5 is two frets, the same as ♭7 to 1.

The seventh flat five chord works well as a passing chord leading from one seventh chord to another. Here is a progression which uses the same seventh flat five shape functioning as two different chords (because of its symmetrical nature):

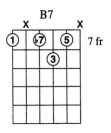

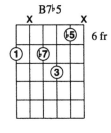

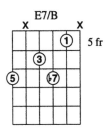

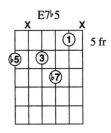

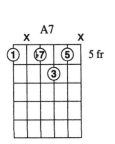

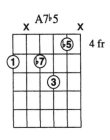

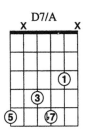

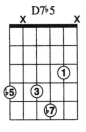

etc....

Diminished Seventh Chord:
1, ♭3, ♭5, ♭♭7

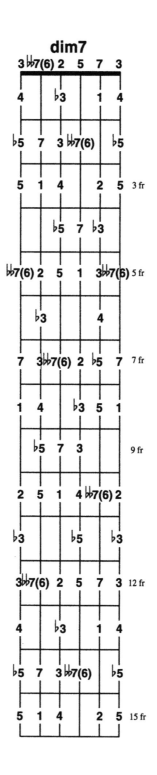

dim7

(Written: C°7, C°, Cdim7, or Cdim)

Directions:

Circle 1, ♭3, ♭5, and ♭♭7 (same as "6"). This gives you all possible C diminished seventh chords, as well as E♭ diminished, G♭ diminished, and B♭♭ (A) diminished chords. As you connect the circles to form "constellations," you will find that the shapes repeat themselves. The diminished seventh chord has the distance of 3 frets from any note to the next. This makes it a symmetrical chord; any note may be considered the root. Because of this, the Cdim can also be called E♭dim (D♯dim), G♭dim (F♯dim), or B♭♭dim (Adim).

There are only three positions for this chord; move up three frets and you have the same position you started with. You may recognize this as the progression used during the chase scenes in the Dudley DooRight cartoon.

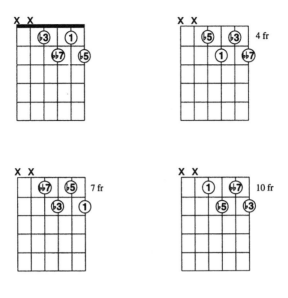

The diminished chord works well as a passing chord, especially if the bass note of the diminished chord is one fret below the bass note of the next chord.

The Diminished Triad
In practical applications, the term "diminished chord" generally refers to the diminished 7th. The *diminished triad* is simply 1, ♭3, and ♭5 without the ♭♭7. It occurs more often in classical music than popular music. You can outline and play some diminished triads by circling the 1, ♭3, and ♭5 in a different color than the ♭♭7.

Suspended Chord: 1, (3), 4, 5

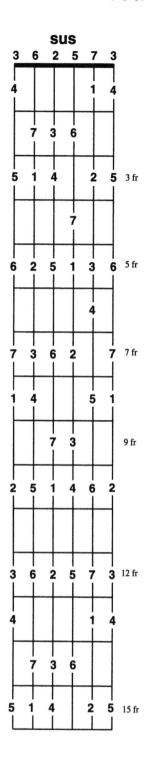

(Written: Csus or Csus4)

Directions:

Circle scale degrees 1, 4, and 5. Place scale degree (3) in parentheses as it is usually left out or placed in a different octave from the "4." This gives you all possible C suspended chords. The suspended chord may be constructed from a major chord by moving the third of the chord (scale degree 3) up one fret.

The suspended chord usually resolves to the major chord; "4" moves back one fret to "3."

Seventh Suspended Chord:
1, (3), 4, (5), 7

7sus

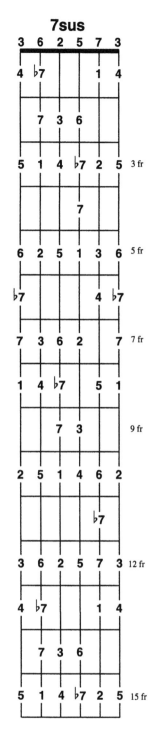

(Written: C7sus, C7sus4)

Directions:

Circle 1, 4, 5 and ♭7. Place (3) in parentheses as it is usually left out or placed in a different octave from the "4." This gives you all possible C seventh suspended chords.

Other types of chords may be "suspended" by adding the fourth degree of the scale. See page 42 (11th chord).

Augmented Chord: 1, 3, ♯5

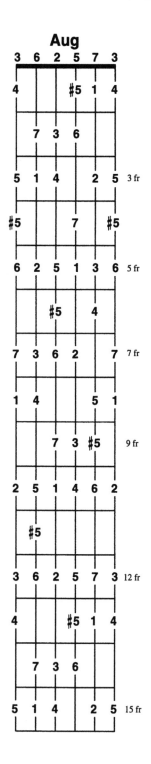

(Written: Caug, C+, or C+5)

Directions:
Circle scale degrees 1, 3, and ♯5. This gives you all possible C augmented chords (also called C augmented 5th).

Seventh Augmented Chord: 1, 3, #5, b7

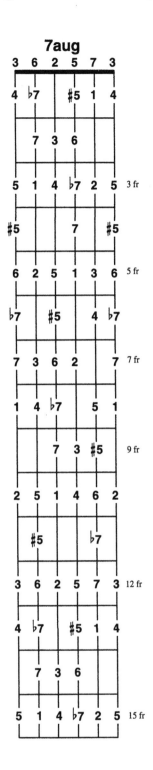

(Written: C7aug, C7#5 or C7+5)

Directions:
Circle 1, 3, #5, and b7. This gives you all possible C seventh augmented chords.

Other types of chords may be augmented by raising (sharping) the fifth degree.

diagram

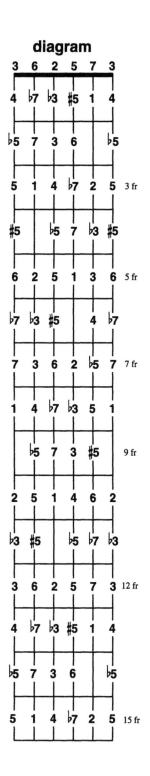

Variations of Seventh Chords

Major Seventh Flat Five Chord: 1, 3, ♭5, and 7.
(Written: Cmaj7(♭5), Cmaj7♭5, CM7-5, C∆7-5)

Major Seventh Augmented Five Chord: 1, 3, ♯5, and 7.
(Written: CMaj7(aug5), CM7+, Cmaj7+5, C∆7+5)

Major Seventh Suspended Chord: 1, 3, 4, (5), and 7.
(Written: Cmaj7sus, Cmaj7sus, CM7sus4, C∆7sus4)

Minor-Major Seventh Flat Five Chord: 1, ♭3, ♭5, and 7.
(Written: Cm(maj7)♭5, Cm(M7)-5)

Minor Seventh Augmented Five Chord: 1, ♭3, ♯5, and ♭7.
(Written: Cm7(aug5), Cm7+, Cm7+5, C-7+5)

Minor Seventh Suspended Chord: 1, ♭3, 4, (5), and ♭7.
(Written: Cmin7sus, Cm7sus4, C-7sus)

Directions:
Using the same methods of chord construction, it is possible to build less common chords. The name of the chord
identifies which chord tones are present in each type of
chord.

Construct for each chord the "A-shape," "E-shape," and "D-
shape." Fill in the chord diagrams on page 31 (Synopsis of
Seventh Chords.)

You may construct complete chord diagrams for any of
these chords in the blank diagram on the facing page.

Minor-Major Seventh Chord:
1, ♭3, 5, 7

m(Maj7)

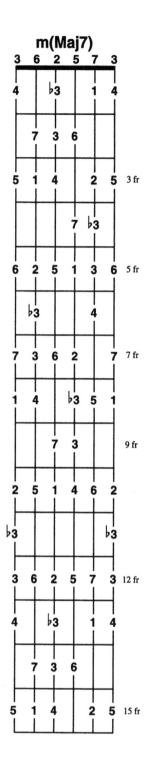

(Written: Cm(maj7), Cm(M7), C-(M7), Cm(△7))

Directions:

This is a minor chord with a major seventh scale degree added. Circle scale degrees 1, ♭3, 5, and 7. This gives you all possible C minor-major seventh chords.

SYNOPSIS OF SEVENTH CHORDS – Exercise

Fill in the following "A-shape" chords with the root on the A string:

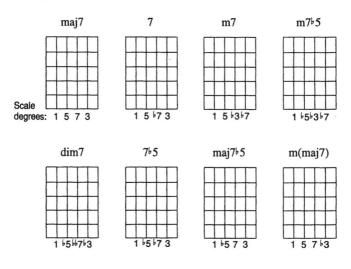

maj7   7   m7   m7♭5

Scale
degrees: 1 5 7 3   1 5 ♭7 3   1 5 ♭3 ♭7   1 ♭5♭3♭7

dim7   7♭5   maj7♭5   m(maj7)

1 ♭5♭♭7♭3   1 ♭5♭7 3   1 ♭5 7 3   1 5 7 ♭3

Fill in the following "E-shape" chords with the root on the E string:

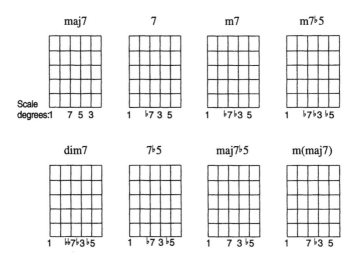

maj7   7   m7   m7♭5

Scale
degrees:1   7 5 3   1   ♭7 3 5   1   ♭7♭3 5   1   ♭7♭3 ♭5

dim7   7♭5   maj7♭5   m(maj7)

1   ♭♭7♭3 ♭5   1   ♭7 3 ♭5   1   7 3 ♭5   1   7 ♭3 5

Fill in the following "D-shape" chords with the root on the D string:

maj7   7   m7   m7♭5

Scale
degrees: 1 5 7 3   1 5 ♭7 3   1 5 ♭7♭3   1 ♭5♭7♭3

dim7   7♭5   maj7♭5   m(maj7)

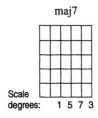
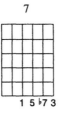
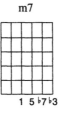

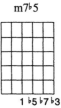

1 ♭5♭♭7♭3   1 ♭5♭7 3   1 ♭5 7 3   1 5 7 ♭3

Sixth Chord: 1, 3, (5), 6

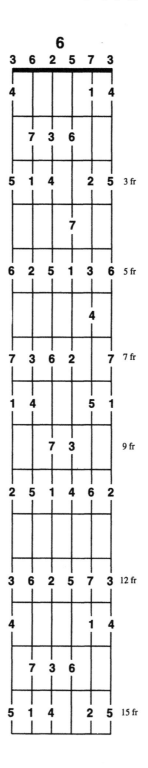

(Written: C6)

Directions:

Circle 1, 3, and 6, and put (5) in parentheses, as "5" is often left out or placed in a different octave from "6." This gives you all possible C sixth chords. You can think of the sixth chord as the major chord with the "5" moved up two frets. Connect the circles to form constellations with "1" in the bass.

Here are some common sixth chord shapes. Find them on the diagram you have completed on the left:

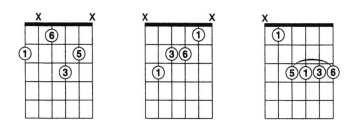

Notice the relationship between C6 and Am7 chords. The only difference is the function of the scale degrees.

The sixth chord forms the same set of shapes on the fingerboard as the minor seventh chord (see page 16), although the notes have different functions (scale degree numbers). The C6 chord may be substituted for Am7, or vice versa. Often chords can have more than one name, simply by changing the function of the notes (making a different scale degree the root).

Minor Sixth Chord: 1, ♭3, (5), 6

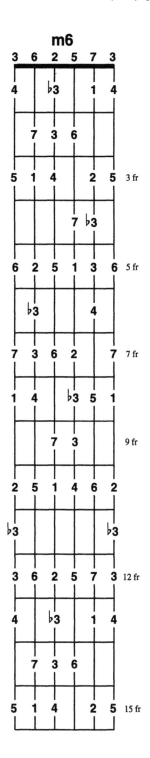

(Written: Cm6 or C-6)

Directions:
Circle 1, ♭3, and 6, and put (5) in parentheses. This gives you all possible C minor sixth chords. Connect the circles to form constellations with "1" in the bass. "5" is optional and generally not used unless it is placed in a different octave from the "6." On the following page are some common minor sixth chord shapes. Find them on the diagram you have completed above.

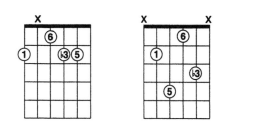

The minor sixth chord forms the same set of shapes on the fingerboard as the minor seventh flat five chord (see page 18), although the notes have different functions. The Cm6 chord may be substituted for Am7♭5 and vice versa. The decision to call a certain chord by one name or the other depends upon the context of the other chords in the progression and/or the bass note.

Here is one harmonization of "Danny Boy" using minor sixth and sixth chords:

DANNY BOY

```
        A       Amaj7
Oh Danny Boy, the pipes, the pipes are

       D6      Dm6
       calling,            from glen to

       A
       glen and down the mountain-

    Esus      E
    side,            the summer's

       A       Amaj7
       gone, and all the flowers are

       D6      Dm6
       dying,          'tis you 'tis

       A       E
       you must go and I must

          D6         A
          bide.
```

Ninth Chord:
1, 3, (5), ♭7, 9 (same as 2)

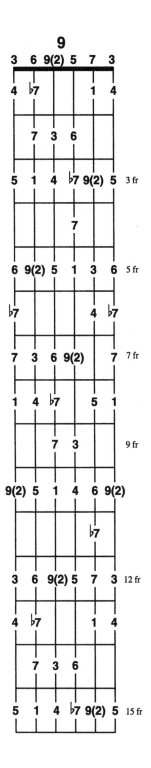

(Written: C9)

Directions:

Circle 1, 3, ♭7, and 9, and put (5) in parentheses. This gives you all possible C ninth chords. The 9th degree of the scale is the same as the 2nd degree of the scale. The term "9" is used instead of "2" to indicate that the dominant 7th is also present in the chord. The 5 is optional and usually left out of the chord because it does not give information essential to identifying the chord. 1 is the root, 3 indicates it is a type of major chord, ♭7 indicates it is a type of dominant seventh chord, and 9 (or 2) identifies it as a 9th chord.

Connect the circles to form constellations with 1 in the bass, 3, ♭7, and 9 in any order. (5) is optional.

You can think of the ninth chord as a seventh chord adding the ninth degree. Here are some convenient ninth chords:

For the first example, flatten out the left hand third finger into a partial bar.

NINTH CHORDS – Exercise
Play the blues progression on page 67 substituting ninth chords for seventh chords. Start one fret below the chord and slide into it.

Add-Nine Chord, Two Chord or Suspended Two Chord:
1, 3, 5, 2 (same as 9)

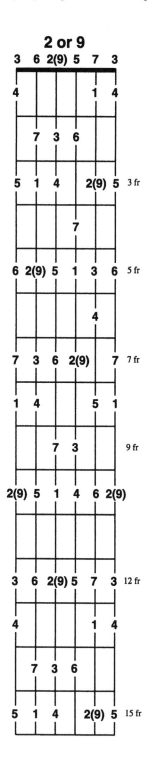

(Written: Cadd9, Cadd2, C2, C(9), or Csus2)

The only difference between the *add-nine* chord and the *ninth* chord is the existence of the dominant 7th (♭7). In modern terminology the Cadd9 chord is also called Cadd2 or Csus2, though a sus2 chord often leaves out the 3rd.

Here are some convenient chord forms. Find them on the complete diagram:

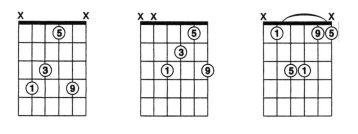

Ninth, sharp-nine, and flat-nine chords:
The ninth, seven flat nine, and seven sharp nine all function as dominant seventh chords. Flat-nine and sharp-nine chords are easy to construct. Just play a ninth chord and move the 9th degree down one fret or up one fret. For fun, try jazzing up some of the seventh chords in the twelve-bar blues progression on page 67 with different types of ninth chords.

To construct all possible seventh flat-nine and seventh sharp-nine chords, fill in the diagrams on the following two pages and connect the circles to form "constellations."

Seventh Flat-Nine Chord:
1, 3, ♭7, ♭9 (same as ♭2)

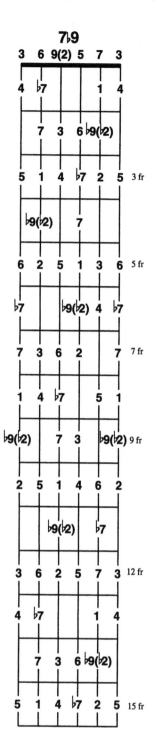

(Written: C7-9, C7♭9, C7(♭9))

Directions:
Circle 1, 3, ♭7, and ♭9 (same as ♭2). Put (5) in parentheses, as it is optional. This will give you all possible C seventh Flat-nine chords.

Seventh Sharp-Nine Chord:
1, 3, ♯7, ♯9 (same as ♯2)

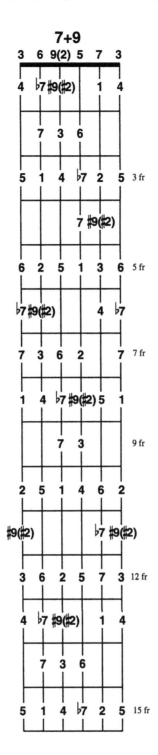

(Written: C7+9, C7♯9, C7(♯9))

Directions:

Circle 1, 3, ♭7, and ♯9 (same as ♯2). Put (5) in parentheses, as it is optional. This will give you all possible C seventh sharp-nine chords.

Eleventh Chord:
1, 3, (5), ♭7, (9), 11 (same as 4)

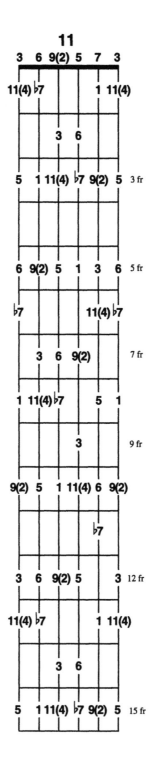

(Written: C11)

Directions:

Circle 1, 3, ♭7, and 11, and put (5) and (9) in parentheses as these notes are optional and often left out of the chord. This gives you all possible C eleventh chords. Connect the circles to form constellations with 1 in the bass, 3, ♭7, and 11 in any order. You may also use 5 and 9.

*When "9" is left out, this is also called the *seventh suspended* chord (C7sus, C7sus4). See page 25.

The eleventh chord may be built from a ninth chord by adding the eleventh degree of the scale (or by moving the 3rd up one fret to the 4th—same as 11th).

Find these eleventh chords on your completed diagram:

Fill in some other chord shapes in the following blank diagrams:

Thirteenth Chord:
1, 3, (5), ♭7, (9), (11), 13

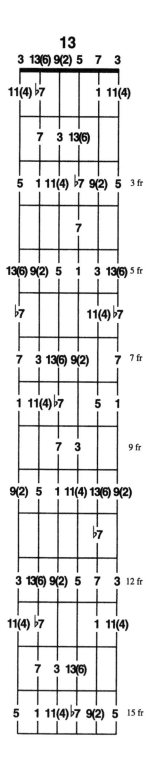

13

(Written: C13)

Directions:

Circle 1, 3, ♭7, and 13 (same as 6). Put 5, 9 (same as 2), and 11 (same as 4) in parentheses as these are optional. This gives you all possible C thirteenth chords. Connect the circles to form constellations with 1 in the bass, 3, ♭7, and 13 in any order. You may also use 5, 9, and 11.

The thirteenth chord may be built from the dominant 7th chord, adding the thirteenth degree (same as the 6th). The difference between a thirteenth chord and a sixth chord is the existence of the ♭7, which defines the chord as a type of dominant chord (wanting to resolve to another chord). Ninth, eleventh, and thirteenth chords may be used as substitutions for seventh chords.

Here are two patterns similar to Paul Simon's accompaniment for the folk song "Scarborough Fair," based around open string chords that form thirteenth and add-nine chords:

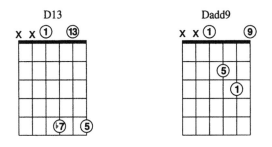

Scarborough Fair Pattern in D -Position:

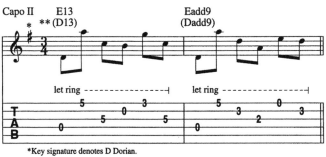

*Key signature denotes D Dorian.

**Symbols in parentheses represent chord names respective to capoed guitar. Symbols above reflect actual sounding chords.

Scarborough Fair Pattern in A -Position:

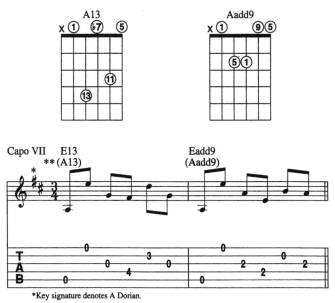

*Key signature denotes A Dorian.

**Symbols in parentheses represent chord names respective to capoed guitar. Symbols above reflect actual sounding chords.

Six-Nine Chord: 1, 3, (5), 6, 9

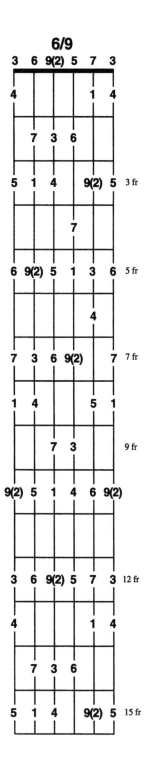

(Written: C6/9, C_9^6)

Directions:

Circle 1, 3, 6, and 9 (same as 2), and put (5) in parentheses as it is optional and often left out of the chord. This gives you all possible C6/9 chords. Connect the circles to form constellations containing the root, 1 (in the bass), at least one 3, 6, and 9 in any order.

Find the 6/9 shape with 1 on the fifth string, 3 on the fourth string, 6 on the third string, and 9 on the second string:

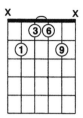

The 6/9 chord is a great ending chord. For a nice effect, start one fret higher and slide back a fret.

Find some other 6/9 chord shapes and fill in on the following blank chord diagrams:

Major Ninth Chord:
1, 3, (5), 7, 9 (same as 2)

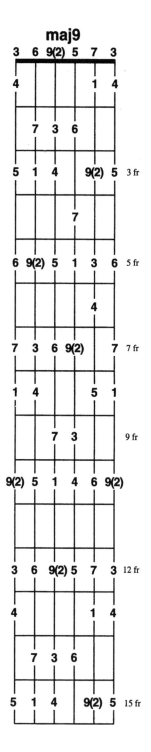

maj9

(Written: Cmaj9, CM9, C△9)

Directions:

Circle degrees 1, 3, 7, and 9 (same as 2) and put (5) in parentheses as it is optional. This gives you all possible C major ninth chords.

Major ninth and major thirteenth chords often make good substitutions for major seventh chords. The major ninth chord consists of a major seventh chord with the 9th degree (same as 2) added.

Major Thirteenth Chord:
1, 3, (5), 7, (9), (11), 13

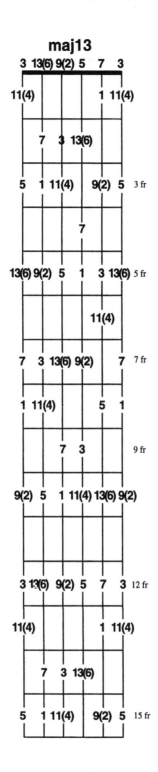

maj13

(Written: Cmaj13, CM13, C△13)

Directions:

Circle degrees 1, 3, 7, and 13 (same as 6) and put (5), (9), and (11) in parentheses. This gives you all possible C major thirteenth chords.

The major thirteenth consists of a major seventh chord with the 13th degree (same as 6) added (the 9th and/or 11th may also be played).

Minor Ninth Chord:
1, ♭3, (5), ♭7, 9

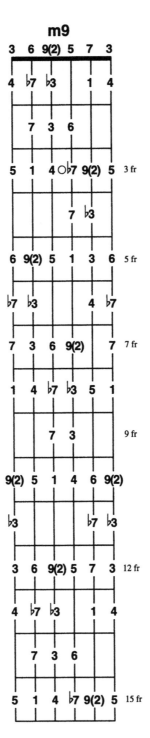

(Written: Cmin9, Cm9, C-9)

Directions:

Circle degrees 1, ♭3, ♭7, and 9 (same as 2) and put (5) in parentheses. This gives you all possible C minor ninth chords.

The minor ninth and minor thirteenth chords often make nice substitutions for minor seventh chords. The minor ninth chord consists of a minor seventh chord with the 9th degree (same as 2) added.

Minor Thirteenth Chord:
1, ♭3, (5), ♭7, (9), (11), 13

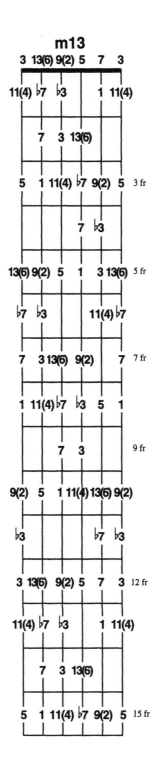

(Written: Cmin13, Cm13, C-13)

Directions:

Circle degrees 1, ♭3, ♭7, and 13 (same as 6) and put (5), (9), and (11) in parentheses. This gives you all possible C minor thirteenth chords.

The minor thirteenth consists of a minor seventh chord with the 13th degree (same as 6) added (the 9th and/or 11th may also be played).

diagram

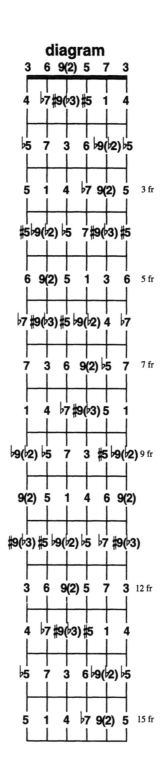

Variations of Ninth Chords:

Major Seventh Flat Nine Chord:
1, 3, (5), 7, and ♭9
(Written: Cmaj7♭9, Cmaj7♭9, C△7-9)

Major Seventh Sharp Nine Chord:
1, 3, (5), 7, and ♯9
(Written: Cmaj7♯9, CM7+9, C△7+9)

Major Ninth Flat Five Chord:
1, 3, ♭5, 7, and 9
(Written: Cmaj9♭5, CM9-5, C△9♭5)

Major Ninth Sharp Five Chord:
1, 3, ♯5, 7, and 9
(Written: Cmaj9♯5, CM9+5, C△9+5)

Minor Seventh Flat Nine Chord:
1, ♭3, (5), ♭7, and ♭9.
(Written: Cm7♭9, Cm7-9, C-7-9)

Minor Ninth Flat Five Chord:
1, ♭3, ♭5, ♭7, and 9.
(Written: Cm9♭5, Cm9-5, C-9-5)

Minor Ninth Sharp Five Chord:
1, ♭3, ♯5, ♭7, and 9.
(Written: Cm9♯5, Cm9+5, C-9+5)

Directions:
Using the same methods of chord construction, you may create complete chord diagrams for any of these chords in the diagram on the facing page.

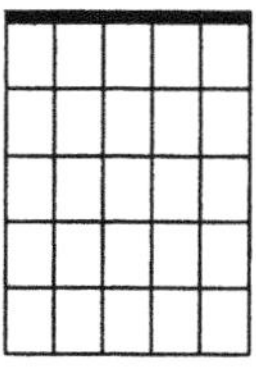

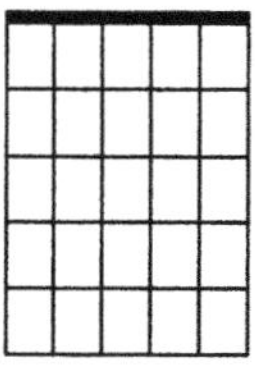

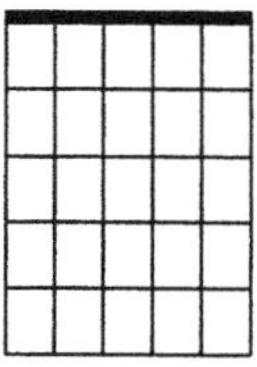

Major Eleventh Chord:
1, 3, (5), 7, (9), 11

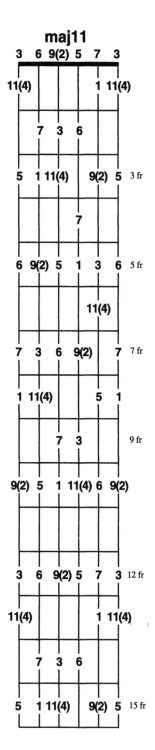

maj11

(Written: Cmaj11, CM11, C△11)

Directions:

Circle degrees 1, 3, 7, and 11 (same as 4) and put (5) and (9) in parentheses. This gives you all possible C major eleventh chords.

When the 9th degree is left out, the major eleventh can also be called the major seventh suspended [M7sus4, maj7sus4, maj7(4)].

Minor Eleventh Chord:
1, ♭3, (5), ♭7, (9), 11

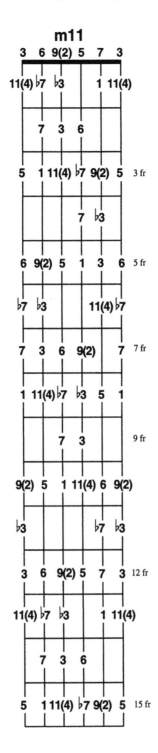

(Written: Cmin11, Cm11, C-11)

Directions:

Circle degrees 1, ♭3, ♭7, and 11 (same as 4) and put (5) and (9) in parentheses. This gives you all possible C minor eleventh chords.

When the 9th degree is left out, the minor eleventh can also be called the minor seventh suspended [m7sus, m7sus4, -7(4)].

TERMINOLOGY: A Discussion of Intervals

Chords can be defined in terms of their relationship to the *major* scale, or in terms of the interval or distance between notes of the chord. For the major chord, the distance between 1 and 3 of the major scale is four frets, or a "major third," between 3 and 5 is three frets, or a "minor third," and between 5 and 1 is five frets, or a "perfect fourth." Here are some musical terms which are commonly used:

The distance of:

1 fret	= minor second	= half step
2 frets	= major second	= whole step
3 frets	= minor third	
4 frets	= major third	
5 frets	= perfect fourth	
6 frets	= diminished fifth or augmented fourth	
7 frets	= perfect fifth	
8 frets	= augmented fifth or minor sixth	
9 frets	= major sixth	
10 frets	= minor seventh	
11 frets	= major seventh	
12 frets	= octave	
13 frets	= minor ninth, or flat nine	
14 frets	= major ninth, or ninth	

Moving the Entire Diagram to Construct All Major Chords

In the same way you moved one chord shape, if you move the entire diagram up one fret you will have all the C# major chords – up two frets gives you all the D major chords. Move the original diagram down one fret and you will have all the B major chords. The pattern of 1-3-5 is the same for all major chords, provided that "1" falls on the name of the chord. Cover up the first three frets of the *Major Chord Diagram* and imagine the neck begins at that point. Now, because all the 1s fall on "A" notes, the diagram depicts all the A major chords. Use the moveable chord guide to make it easier to visualize the moveable diagram. The shapes all repeat themselves after twelve frets, so the diagrams can be extended infinitely. All diagrams that you will construct in this book may be moved the same way.

Chord Shapes

Diagram some basic major chord shapes on the following page and label where "1" is located in each shape. Notice where these shapes are located in the complete *Major Chord Diagram* and in relation to the other shapes. Pay attention to which string contains the root of the chord in each shape. It is usually the first note you play in the bass. Sometimes instead of fingering and strumming the entire chord, it is more practical to play only a few notes of the chord, either plucking the strings or skipping over a string with the pick. It is helpful to learn the names of the notes on the 6th and 5th strings so that you can quickly play one of the chord shapes on the correct fret to make any desired chord. The exercises in this book will help you to gradually memorize where each of the scale degrees are located in each shape.

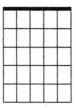

Barre Chords

Where there are several scale degrees located on the same fret it is often convenient to bar across with one finger, usually the index finger. In order for all the notes to ring out with the least amount of pressure, position the bar very close to the fret. Instead of playing on the pad of the finger, position the index finger more on the side closest to the thumb. Concentrate on applying pressure only on the strings that are needed in the chord. Usually there is no need to apply pressure equally all the way across the bar.

Moving Chord Shapes

You can use the *Major Chord Diagram* to find all of the major chords. Move any shape on the complete C *Major Chord Diagram* up one fret and it will become a C♯ major chord. Place a given chord shape so that scale degree "1" falls upon a D note, and it becomes a D chord. In other words, you need only know one shape in order to make any major chord. Whatever note "1" falls upon is the root, or the name of the chord.

For example, take the "E-shape":

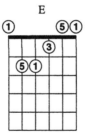

Move it up to the first fret so that the "1" on the sixth string falls on an F and it becomes an F major chord:

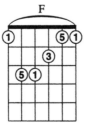

*Remember, when moving chord positions that contain open strings, those strings do not remain open, but must be fretted to maintain the same intervallic relationship (unless these open strings are desired scale degrees in the new chord. (When changing from an E Major chord to an F Major chord, the first, second, and sixth strings that were open must now be fretted at the 1st fret. This is done by placing the first finger all the way across the first fret to form a barre chord).

Move the same shape up to the second fret and it becomes an F♯ Major chord, to the third fret it becomes a G Major chord, to the 8th fret it becomes a C Major chord, etc.

Any chord shape may be moved up or down the neck to make other chords of the same "quality" (major, minor, etc.) provided you don't play any open strings which are not scale degrees of the chord. Take the D chord shape and slide it up one fret. Play only the first, second, and third strings. This now becomes a D♯ chord. Move it up one more fret and it becomes an E chord.

A Look at Scale Construction...How and Why This System Works!

The reason that this works for *all* chords is that the distances between the notes stay the same for respective chords and scales.

Labeling the notes, or positions, on the guitar fingerboard as numbers instead of letters makes it easier to define and build all types of chords. The *major scale*, in particular the C major scale, is used throughout this book to build all chords in all positions. The same patterns work for all other keys.

Since all of the notes repeat themselves at the 12th fret, we can envision the fingerboard as moving infinitely in both directions, or as a loop connecting at the 12th fret.

Scales and chords are both defined by the intervals between the notes. The major scale is a series of seven notes arranged in a pattern of whole steps (distance of two frets) and half steps (distance of one fret). The first note of the scale is the name of the scale (called the root, or tonic). We can build any major scale using this formula:

Major Scale Formula

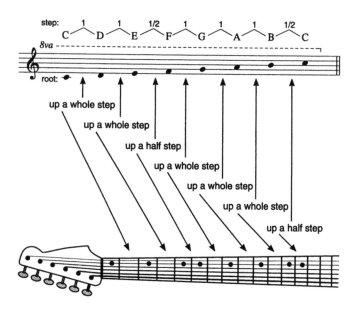

The scale ends on the same letter name as the first note (the root), one octave higher.

Using the Capo to Transpose

The capo may be used to easily transpose a song into any key. The capo works the same way as your index finger bar. If you are playing in a given key (the key of C for example) and wish to play in another key, place the capo on the first fret (finger the chords normally as though the capo were the end of your guitar) and you are now playing in the key a half step higher (the key of C#). For each fret the capo is moved up, the key moves up another half step. Conversely, if you wish to transpose another position into the key of C, find a C chord in the shape or position you wish to play in—the A-shape in third position, for example. Put the capo on the 3rd fret and play as though in the key of A. In reality, you will be playing in the key of C.

The Circle of Fifths

The interval of a perfect fifth is an important building block to music as we know it. Aside from the unison and the octave, the fifth is the most consonant interval occurring in nature. (The natural harmonic occurring at the 7th fret, exactly 1/3 of the string length, is a fifth higher than the first harmonic at the 12th fret, exactly 1/2 of the string length.) As a result, when we organize notes in order one fifth higher than the next, we have many patterns that occur (Fascinating for those of us with an interest in math!). In our equal temperament tuning system we eventually go through all 12 tones and end up at the same note where we started (although several octaves higher, the octave of the note is not important in this theoretical model). The circle of fifths can be used, among other things, as a quick reference to determine how many sharps or flats occur in a given key.

Circle of Fifths Diagram from "Building Guitar Arrangements from the Ground Up"

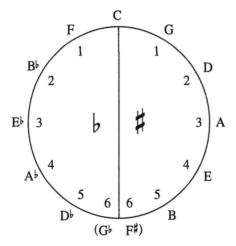

The number inside the circle indicates the number of sharps or flats in the major key just outside the circle.

The "order of sharps" goes around the circle of fifths: F#-C#-G#-D#-A#-E#-B#.

The "order of flats" goes backwards around the circle of fifths: Bb-Eb-Ab-Db-Gb-Cb-Fb.

For example, the key with three sharps (key of A major) will have the *first* three in the "order of sharps": F#, C# and G#. The key with two flats (key of Bb major) will have the *first* two flats in the "order of flats": Bb and Eb.

Exercise on Inversions – Major Chords

You will find that there are three different combinations of 1, 3, and 5 on each set of adjacent strings. Practice moving from one inversion to the next on the 1st, 2nd, and 3rd strings, then on each other set of adjacent strings. Try to visualize the larger shape around the triad you are playing. Think of the "C-A-G-E-D" chord shapes.

A chord with 1 in the bass is called *root position*. A chord with 3 in the bass is called the *first inversion*, and a chord with 5 in the bass is called the *second inversion:*

C Major Inversions

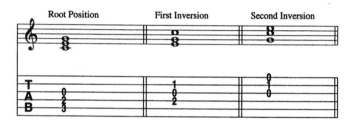

Using One Shape to Find All Major Chords

Use one shape (the "E-shape") to play all the chords in "Amazing Grace." Then use two different shapes, depending on which is more convenient or sounds better. Use the "E-shape" for chords with the root on the 6th string and the "A-shape" for chords with the root on the 5th string.

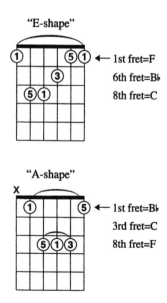

Amazing Grace

C F C
Amazing Grace, how sweet the sound
C G
That saved a wretch like me
C F C
I once was lost but now am found
*(Am) G C
Was blind but now I see.

*optional

Finding New Chord Positions

Now play the chords to "Amazing Grace" in *third* position (starting on the third fret). If playing with another guitarist, you can create an instant harmony simply by playing the same chords in a different position. Learn to change back and forth between these chords easily so that you can use this same position again later. Think of the chords in terms of I, IV, and V chords. If you were playing in the key of C♯ you could use the same chord shapes; simply move the entire progression up one fret.

C

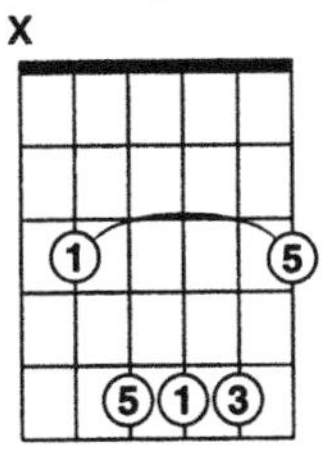

G

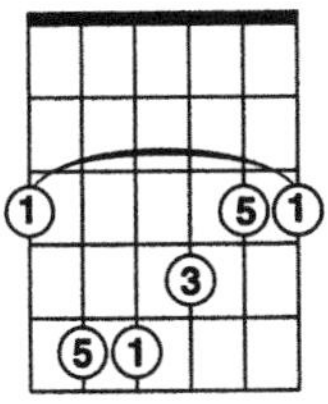

F

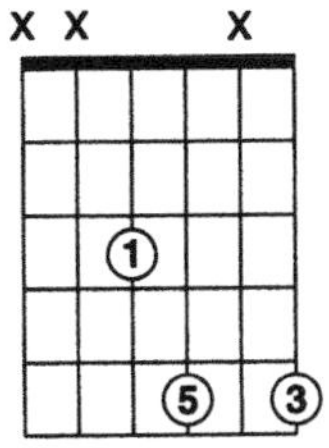

For an extra challenge, find and play the C, F, and G chords in fifth position or eighth position.

Another Way to Look at the Minor Chord Diagram:

You may already be familiar with some of the minor chord shapes. Find a shape that you recognize as Am. Cover up the first three frets of the diagram so that the shape is on the correct fret to make an Am chord. Notice that all the 1s fall on "A" notes, so the diagram depicts all the A minor chords.

You can also construct minor chords as 1, 3, and 5 of the minor scale. This will yield exactly the same *Minor Chord Diagram.* The notes of the minor scale surrounding the chords may also be helpful for the purpose of improvising melodies around minor chords. The minor scale is constructed: whole-half-whole-whole-half-whole-whole. (Or you can construct the minor scale by starting on the 6th note of the relative major scale. It contains the same notes as that relative major scale.

Here are some major and minor chords. Remember that all shapes that don't contain open strings (or in which you only play the fretted notes) may be moved anywhere on the neck. The shape determines whether it's major or minor (the quality of the chord) and the 1 in the chord always falls on the letter name (root) of the chord.

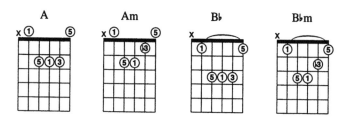

(same shape as B♭m; 2nd fret Bm, 3rd fret Cm, 4th fret C#m, 5th fret Dm, 6th fret D#m, etc.)

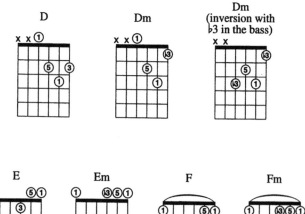

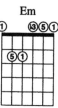

An Observation About Two Shapes of Barre Chords:

You may notice that, when forming a barre chord with the root on the 6th, or E string, it has an "E-shape." In other words, the major chord form looks like an E chord with a bar (or capo), and the minor chord form looks like an Em chord with a bar. Likewise, the barre chord with the root on the 5th, or A-string, has an A-shape. This makes it easy to find any major or minor chord at two different positions on the guitar, provided you know the names of the notes on the 6th and 5th strings. Whatever note your index finger bar points to (on the 5th or 6th string) is the name of the chord.

Some shapes may be difficult or impossible to reach. In this case, it may be possible to play just a smaller part of the chord (on 3 or 4 strings). Be careful to accurately judge the number of frets between notes in a chord diagram.

Here are some different ways to play chords in the key of B minor:

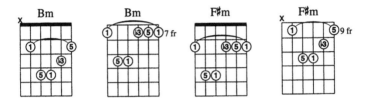

Scarborough Fair

Bm		F#m	Bm

Are you going to Scarborough Fair

D   Bm   E   Bm

Parsley sage, rosemary and thyme

Bm   D   A

Remember me to one who lives there

Bm   A   Bm

She once was a true love of mine.

You may also use the following (upper position) open string chords:

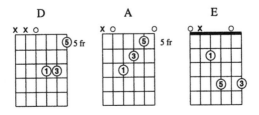

Power Chords

Rock guitarists often play chords that do not contain the 3rd degree of the scale. You may remember, that when constructing the minor chords on page 10, the 3rd determines whether the chord is major or minor. Leaving the third out gives the chord an ambiguous sound, and it can be used for either a major or minor chord.

The three lowest notes in the "E-shape" (either major or minor) look like this:

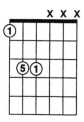

and the three lowest notes in the "A-shape" (either major or minor) look like this:

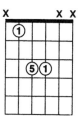

Notice that they are the same shape but on different strings, and neither contains the third of the chord. When playing these chords, muffle the open strings with the left hand to be sure to play only the three fretted strings:

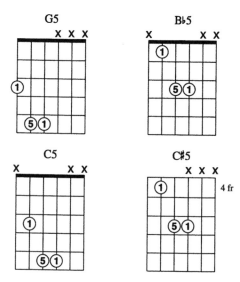

"Smoke" Progression

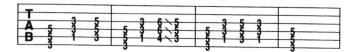

Open String Chords

The first, third, and sixth strings of the C Major chord may be played open because they are chord tones (1, 3, or 5 in the scale). Experiment with playing C chords up the neck while leaving the first and/or third strings open. Other chords may use open strings as well (where the chord tones fall on fret number zero).

A Word About the "Number System" or the "Harmonized Scale"

Chords built upon each of the notes of the scale are often called by number names just as the notes of the scale are called by number names. This allows a song to be transposed into any key almost instantaneously. In standard classical music notation, chords are written in Roman numerals, sometimes with minor chords and diminished chords in lower case. In modern popular music (in Nashville in particular), this system is widely used with regular Arabic numbers for the chords. A minus (-) sign after the number indicates a minor chord.

To build a "harmonized scale," simply create triads on every note of the scale, building a chord upon each note. Seventh chords and ninth chords can also be built by continuing to add thirds upon each chord. The types of chords derived on each scale degree (major, minor, diminished) will be the same respectively for any key:

	(ii)	(iii)			(vi)	(vii)
I	II	III	IV	V	VI	VII
1	2-	3-	4	5	6-	7-
C	Dm	Em	F	G	Am	B°

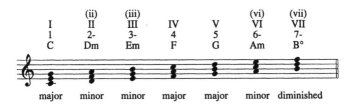

| major | minor | minor | major | major | minor | diminished |

The chords used most often in all forms of western music are the I, IV, and V chords in any key. You can see that these are the major chords when the scale is harmonized.

Position Playing

Here are the I, IV, and V7 chords in one position. (The V chord is often played as a dominant seventh.) All three chords start on the same fret, and "1" falls on the name of the chord.

If this is the I chord:
("1" falls on the name of the chord and the name of the key)

The IV chord is:
(Don't play the second string.)

And the V7 chord is:

These shapes can be useful in playing the I, IV, and V7 chords in all keys. Simply keep the same special relationships between the three chords. For example, play these chords on the third fret as written and you have the I, IV, and V7 chords in the key of C; the I chord is C, the IV chord is F, and the V7 chord is G7. One fret higher you have the I, IV, and V7 chords in the key of C♯. Play these chords on the fifth fret and you have the I, IV, and V7 chords in the key of D: the I chord is D, the IV chord is G, and the V7 chord is A7.

The blues uses seventh chords for all three: I7, IV7, and V7.

The 12-Bar Blues

Use the moveable "E-shape" seventh chord to play all chords in the following blues progression. Then try using the "A-shape" seventh chord and/or the "C-shape" seventh chord. Find these chord shapes on the complete Seventh Chord diagram on page 12.

Strum four beats per chord symbol.

Blues in C

C7	F7	C7	C7
F7	F7	C7	C7
G7	F7	C7	C7(G7)

"E-shape" 7th chord

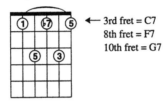

1st fret = F7
3rd fret = G7
8th fret = C7

"A-shape" 7th chord

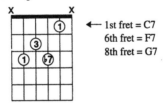

3rd fret = C7
8th fret = F7
10th fret = G7

"C-shape" 7th chord

1st fret = C7
6th fret = F7
8th fret = G7

Play the 12-bar blues in other keys using the number system.

I7	IV7	I7	I7
IV7	IV7	I7	I7
V7	IV7	I7	I7(V7)

Here are some other common seventh chord shapes. Find them on your complete *Dominant Seventh Chord Diagram* (p. 12) and practice the 12-bar blues progression using these chord shapes.

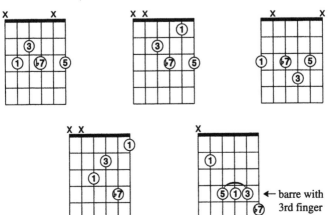

← barre with 3rd finger

"A-Shape" Chords

Once you understand the concept of chord construction, take one new chord shape at a time and integrate it into your playing. Use the new chord shape at every possible occasion until it becomes part of your musical vocabulary.

The following chart is a way to expand upon one chord shape using your knowledge of chord construction. Using just this one major shape and its minor, seventh, and major seventh counterparts, you will be able to play any major, minor, seventh, or major seventh chord simply by placing the shape on different frets. Because the root is on the A string, we nickname this the "A-shape."

Major   minor

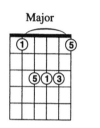   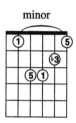

7th   Major 7th

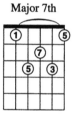

If you are not already familiar with the names of the notes on the 5th string, now is the time! You already know that the 3rd fret is C because it is the bass note for the C chord, and you already know that the 5th fret is a D because that is where you tune the guitar, so two frets higher will be E, and one fret higher than that (on the 8th fret) is F (because there is no sharp between E and F). At the 12th fret all notes repeat themselves, so you're back to A, and two frets lower than that (the 10th fret) is G.

Try playing this song using only the "A-shapes" up and down the fingerboard. (The Am may be played in first position.)

House of the Rising Sun

Am   C   D Fmaj7
There is a house in New Orleans
  Am   C E E7
They call the Rising Sun
 Am   C D   F
It's been the ruin of many a poor boy
   Am E Am E7
And me I know I'm one.

Expanding upon the "A-shape"

Using only the middle strings (5, 4, 3, and 2), play each of the following chords. Notice where the scale degrees are located. Notice that for each type of seventh chord in this series, one note of the chord moves back one fret from the previous chord. The first and sixth strings are not to be played; the first string may be easily muted by the left hand.

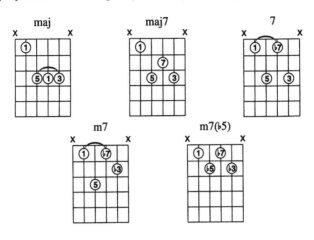

Looking ahead in the sequence... The diminished seventh differs from the half-diminished seventh (also called the minor seventh flat-five) in that the 7th degree is flatted twice in the full diminished seventh.

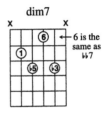

dim7

← 6 is the same as ♭♭7

Example:

This is a progression that can be used against the melody of "Ain't Misbehavin'." Strum twice per chord. This progression sounds good with all down-strokes, releasing the pressure of the left hand quickly after strumming the chord to produce very short, almost muffled chords.

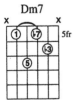

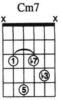
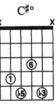

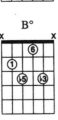
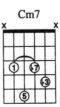
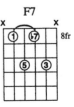

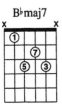
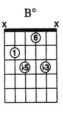
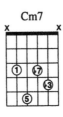
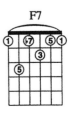

69

Glossary of Terms and Chord Definitions

Enharmonic = Two names for the same note, such as A♯ and B♭.

Flat = flat, or minor (when following letter name)= ♭ (lower the note one fret)

(–) = flat, or minor (when following letter name)

Minor = m (flat the third degree of the chord)

Sharp = ♯ (raise the note one fret)

(+) = sharp, or augmented (when following a letter name)

Augmented = aug (sharp, or sharp the 5th degree of the chord)

Diminished = dim or ° (Triad with a minor 3 and flat 5; for a diminished seventh chord, add a double-flatted seventh to a diminished triad; a major interval reduced by a whole step, or a minor or perfect interval reduced by a half step.)

Suspended = sus = 4 (Add the fourth degree or raise the third degree (one fret) to the fourth degree.)

Triad = Any variety of scale degrees 1, 3, and 5. These are the basic types of triads:

> Major = Maj = M = Chord letter name without other indications (1, 3, 5)
>
> Minor = min = m = (–) (1, ♭3, 5)
>
> Augmented = aug = + = +5 = ♯5 (1, 3, ♯5)
>
> Diminished Triad = dim = ° (1, ♭3, ♭5)

Usually the word (triad) is written after the diminished chord to indicate that just these three scale degrees are desired. Otherwise, it is generally assumed that the dim7 (°7) chord is to be played.

Variations to the triad:
Suspended = sus = sus4 = 4 (1, 4, 5 or 1, 3, 4, 5)
The third degree may also be played, although it sounds better in a different octave than the fourth degree.

The fifth degree may be left out of the following chords:

Sixth = 6 (1, 3, 5, 6)

Minor Sixth = m6 (1, ♭3, 5, 6)

Add Nine = (9) = 2 (1, 3, 5, 9 which is the same as 1, 3, 5, 2)

Six-Nine = 6/9 (1, 3, 5, 6, 9)

Types of Seventh Chords = Any variety of scale degrees 1, 3, 5, and 7. The name of the chord indicates which scale degrees make up the chord. If the fifth degree of a given seventh chord is not altered (sharped or flatted), the fifth may be left out without greatly changing the overall quality of the chord.

These are the basic types of seventh chords:

Major Seventh = Maj7 = M7 = $\triangle$7 (1, 3, 5, 7)

Seventh = dominant seventh = 7 (1, 3, 5, $\flat$7)

Minor Seventh = min7 = m7 = -7 (1, $\flat$3, 5, $\flat$7)

Half Diminished Seventh = $\emptyset$7 = Minor Seventh Flat Five = m7($\flat$5) = m7-5 (1, $\flat$3, $\flat$5, $\flat$7)

Diminished Seventh = dim7 = $^\circ$7 = Diminished = dim = $^\circ$ (Usually implies the seventh chord) 1, $\flat$3, $\flat$5, $\flat\flat$7 which is the same as... 1, $\flat$3, $\flat$5, 6 (A double flatted 7th is the same as a 6th).

Using the definitions you have learned you can also construct the following seventh chords:

Seventh Flat Five = 7($\flat$5) = 7-5 (1, 3, $\flat$5, $\flat$7)

Major Seventh Flat Five = Maj7($\flat$5) = $\triangle$7-5 (1, 3, $\flat$5, 7)

Minor Major Seventh = m(maj7) = m$\triangle$7 (1, $\flat$3, 5, 7)

Seventh Augmented = 7+ = 7(+5) = 7($\sharp$5) (1, 3, $\sharp$5, $\flat$7)

Seventh Suspended = 7sus = 7(sus4) (1, 3, 4, 5, $\flat$7)

Major Seventh Suspended = $\triangle$7sus (1, 3, 4, 5, 7)

The following extended chords function the same way as (and can be substituted for) their relative seventh chords. [Scale degree 9 is the same as 2, 11 is the same as 4, 13 is the same as 6.] It is acceptable to leave out scale degree 5 and scale degrees between but not including 7 and the highest scale degree number in the chord, without greatly changing the quality of the chord. The third tells if the chord is major or minor. The seventh is what distinguishes a 9th chord from an add-nine chord and an 11th chord from a suspended chord.

Ninth = 9 (1, 3, 5, $\flat$7, 9)

Major Ninth = maj9 = $\triangle$9 (1, 3, 5, 7, 9)

Minor Ninth = m9 (1, $\flat$3, 5, $\flat$7, 9)

Seventh Flat Nine = 7($\flat$9) = 7-9 (1, 3, 5, $\flat$7, $\flat$9)

Seventh Sharp Nine = 7($\sharp$9) = 7+9 (1, 3, 5, $\flat$7, $\sharp$9)

Eleventh = 11 (1, 3, 5, $\flat$7, 9, 11)

Major Eleventh = maj11 = $\triangle$11 (1, 3, 5, 7, 9, 11)
(If you don't play the 9, this can also be called $\triangle$7sus).

Thirteenth = 13 (1, 3, 5, $\flat$7, 9, 11, 13)

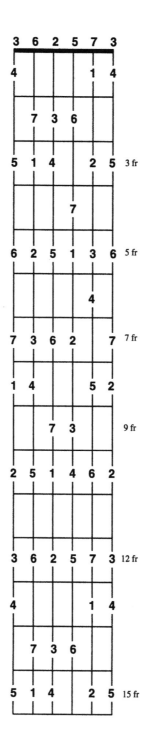

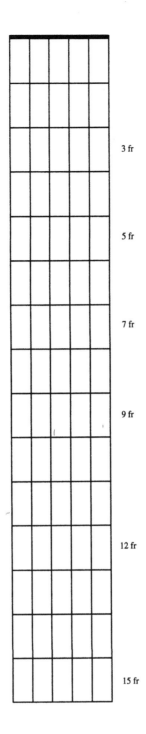

3 fr

5 fr

7 fr

9 fr

12 fr

15 fr

About the Author:

Muriel Anderson, author of Hal Leonard's *Building Guitar Arrangements from the Ground Up* and winner of the 1989 National Fingerpicking Guitar Championship, has been acclaimed as "the premier woman fingerstyle guitarist of our day." She has released several recordings on CGD Music: *Heartstrings, Arioso From Paris, Hometown Live, A Little Christmas Gift,* and a duet CD with guitarist Jean-Felix Lalanne on Rarified Records entitled *Le Duet.* In 1993, *Heartstrings* traveled 2.5 million miles, accompanying the astronauts into orbit on a Space Shuttle mission. Muriel Anderson writes for *Acoustic Musician, Fingerstyle Guitar* and *Guitar Player* magazines. Between recording and touring, Muriel teaches guitar at Wheaton College in Illinois and Belmont College in Nashville.

Check out Muriel Anderson's home page at
http://www.teleport.com/~richm/muriel.html

Moveable Chord Guide

Cut out this Moveable Chord Guide and remove the center section (or you may photocopy onto stiff paper or transparency). Slide along the chord diagrams you have constructed to instantly transpose the chords. The letters along the left side are the names of the notes on the sixth string. Slide the chord guide until scale degree "1" on the sixth string lines up with the desired letter name. You will then see every possible way to make that chord in every position. Remember that the notes and chord shapes repeat themselves at the twelfth fret, so the diagrams can be extended infinitely.

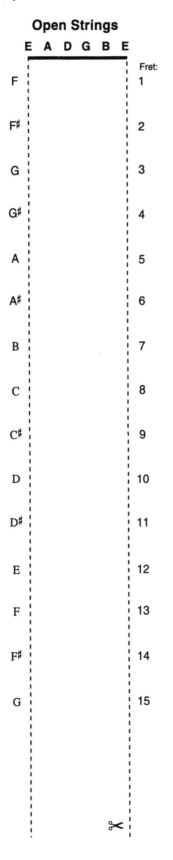